SUN, SAND & SALT

Collected Writings from a Green Mind

By

Jason A. Safford

At the foot of wisdom,
the soul finds love
where fools perish

Table of Contents

About Sun, Sand and Salt 9

SUN 13
    Sunshine 14
    Joy 14
    Sunset on the Jetty Rocks 15
    Alone with the Stars 15
    Artemis 17
    True Beauty 18
    Meditation in the Park 19
    Grace 20
    Faith 21
    At the top 22
    Athena 23
    Valentine 26
    Foundation 27
    Happiness 27
    A walk under the moon 28
    Riddle of Love 29
    Love remains 30
    The Philosophers Stone 32

Catching Victory 33

SAND 43

The Crown 44

Torture 45

Naked Arms 46

The pulchritude of a tumultuous cryptic enigma
called my mind 47

Snow drifts 48

Trees without leaves 49

Death of a Child 50

Grief 51

Atlas humbled 52

The Burden of lies 53

So in love 54

Black Consideration 56

Vacation Nightmare 58

SALT 75

Heavenly Bonds 76

Your Mind 76

Want 79

Missing You 80

Possession 82

Wet 83

Your Kiss 85

Reflection 85

Tears 86

Saudade 86

My love that you're running from 88

Passion 91

Thundershowers 92

Submission 93

Your lips 94

Communication 95

The worth of your mind 96

7 words 97

True Love 100

Bonaparte and Clementine crash in the French Quarter 103

About Sun, Sand and Salt

I fell in love with the written word unexpectedly, when I was 15, sitting in Ms. Gold's Poetry class. The next year she introduced me to expository writing and I was still somewhat adverse to the writing form, but the free-writing approach of her class launched me on a path that I have continued to pursue with increasing passion.

Spending my childhood summers on the rocky beach of Wading River, Long Island, I would enjoy the gritty pain of walking barefoot on the hot stones and burning sand, which the blazing Sun had beaten into submission all morning. Cooling my poor scorched toes in the salt water of the Long Island sound would be the only recourse, to alleviate the throbbing in my feet, while I felt the powerful rays of the Sun on my bleached hair and back. As I got older, I began to help my father with fixing and repairing our summer home, doing the constant maintenance that was always required with owning a beachfront property. He would explain in his thoughtful and insightful way that Sun, Sand and Salt are the three elements of nature that you cannot overcome, they will wear you down over time and they are pervasive in everything.

Sun, Sand and Salt is a collection of my writings over the past 25 years that are focused on life, personal experiences and observations and expressions of my Green mind. Being actively involved in the development of the Green industry for the past 18 years, I am appropriating the word Green in conjunction with my mind because of my greater understanding of how I have incorporated Green within my writing and overall thought process.

As I am also a speaker and have a platform called "Develop Your Green Mind" it's fitting that I have called this book a collection of writings from a Green Mind. Simply put, a Green Mind is one that self-actualizes its goals and positively impacts the world around it to achieve and surpass those goals creating a more powerful result for everyone involved.

Organized in three individual sections, the Sun section, which is the energy of our life, represents the happiness of life, the joy, the pleasure and the euphoria. The Sand section, which is the power of life, represents the grit of life, the toughness, the hardships and the pain. The Salt section, which is the love of life, represents the passion of life, the musty feelings, the erotic pleasure and the overwhelming energy of love.

In organizing and compiling these writings together in one book, my goal is to give the reader an ability to examine freely the different thoughts, ideas and feelings based on their own needs and moods at that moment. Mirroring or reflecting those moods and needs or bringing stark contrast to their current experience. In so doing, this book becomes a sustainable resource that continually provides energy, power and love as needed to impact the reader positively, thereby stimulating a greener mind. My hope is that the impact of this book on you, the reader, is far greater than anything I could have imagined in writing it. Happy reading!

Jason A. Safford

SUN

When we imagine the greatest moments of happiness in our life, they are often described with a gleam in our eye and a radiant sunshine in our description of the details. The Sun is our energy source. It brings life and light to everything on earth. How we use its power, how we are inspired by its rising and setting each day, these are the awesome choices we have to warm our thoughts and ideas. This section is focused on the energy, enthusiasm and happiness that makes the sun seem brighter and translates what all its brilliant powerful light brings to our earth. As Martin Luther King, Jr. once stated, "Darkness cannot drive out darkness; only light can do that."

Sunshine

Underneath cornflower blue
Exposed completely feeling warm
Eyes afraid to look at you
Burning me all the way through

Now so powerful is your form
Incredible is your light
Less clouds gather in a swarm
Disruption only with thunderstorm

More a smile incomparable bright
Fixed in perfect day
Gleaming greater than teeth white
On horizons lips til the night

Setting low to hide away
Glistening in water's bliss
I bid goodnight until new day
And seal it with a kiss to stay

***

Joy

Dawn brims with excitement as she smiles
The hues of sunrise radiate from her lips
Serenity pulls magnetically in her eyes
Colorful canvas of painted sky her stare rips

Sunset on the Jetty Rocks

Seafoam tops on curling waves
Dancing joyfully in golden rays
Distract the focus of admiring gaze
On the opulent hues of blue horizon

Crashing on the jetty rocks
Waves join the symphony with seagull flocks
Conducted by a wind that mocks
Before the footprints of a brilliant moon risin'

From on high the darkness met
Exquisite drops of Poseidon wet
Glistening from a golden purple sunset
All the world does she enliven

***

Alone with the Stars

Looking up at the stars tonight
I saw a million sparkling lights
But there was a void when I looked for my favorite constellation

It is not that it was not there
I just could not see it clear
Like it was trying to hide from me, perhaps playfully

It was a beautiful day today
I took a walk on the beach and swam away
I smiled and laughed in the shining sun

The sunset tonight was heart-stopping
Striations of every hue blasted across the sky
Overwhelming me with thoughts of your smile

Now I sit underneath the stars
Wondering how you are
Wanting to know what future there may be
I'm floating in limbo
Totally steered by faith
Navigating my mind and my emotions by love alone

The communication I so crave
Wanting desperately to have again
Connecting with your mind on our own plane

Partners in crime
Mastering our minds
life together always and forever

Is what I feel
A celestial bond
Connecting our souls

All these thoughts overwhelm me
Wishing that we will be together

This is how I connect with you as I sit alone with the stars

***

Artemis

Elegance pervades her every step
Soft lips capture delicate beauty
Gentle hands veil a firm touch
Strong posture resonates
Her eyes fixed determination

Her prey is unknowing of her stare
Subtle looks disguised
She stalks without moving
Sizing up each movement
inhaling physical features
Climate surrounding tells her everything

In her eyes are sapphires of passion
Bringing resolute dreams
She carries karats of wisdom like a fashion
From her shoulders confidence gleams

***

True Beauty

Imagine the view from the eyes of The Creator
Above the world on highest peaks
Or surrounded by the vastness of the ocean
Setting sun streaming tears down your cheeks

Deep inside the lushest forest it grows
Where poets dare aspire
Or grand music halls where the greatest play
With unbridled passion and desire

None compares to the treasure of
A mother's first glimpse of child
Such gift from the power above
See lone flower on top the mountain wild

More beautiful than sunset after hurricane
Or before the maelstrom, a rising sun
When the colors you never see show brightest
And our imagination begins to run

Like paint strokes on Autumn leaves
Across the Adirondacks
Color and hue brushed by the Almighty
In never-ending climax

Only the child who shares his toy
Getting an epiphany in that time
Can understand the meaning
Of something so sublime

Such power cannot be contained
Nor bottled or captured in any pleasure
Neither freezing for any moment
True Beauty is a timeless treasure

***

Meditation in the Park

I took my daily walk today
In the local park walkway
Starting south and towards the sun
Crossing paths with those who run

Around the pond and across the creek
The pathways are there for those who seek
With imposing trees that stretch high above
Their branches reaching out with love

And far beyond shows the bluest sky
Keeping contrast in my eye
Against the green of the grass
My thoughts wandering to memories past

With each step I move ahead
More vigorously striding around the watershed
Catching glimpses of park residents who scurry
Bustling about for winters hurry

There, in that moment, I take my breath

Reflecting on all the living and untimely death
Leaves falling from the trees
Life without the birds and bees

Chirping sounds quell my mind
Soothing thoughts help me unwind
I breathe deeply and catch my thought
Grabbing zipper and pulling taught

Briskly then I walk again
A joyful smile directed from my brain
Life reminders all around me stark
As I walk alone meditating in this park

***

Grace

So gentle are her words
Even when she corrects you
Kindness is the armor with which she protects herself

***

Faith

Each day the silence rings in my ears
A constant reminder chimes
Your smile is not available

Walking around the park
Searching my soul
Waiting in limbo knowing I know nothing

I try sending you my thoughts
Wondering if you are receiving them openly
Hoping they are not discarded without regard

It must be hard
Not allowing yourself to communicate
Keeping your distance

There is no distance between us
No matter how many miles apart we are
My mind is yours

I feel our connection
Every waking minute
Undeterred in its focus regardless of distraction

The sound of your voice
The smell of your scent
The light of your smile

I know it won't be long

Until then I carry on
Led by a growing sense of faith

Our connection will renew again
This time stronger

***

At the top

Standing tall
Above it all
I see the world below me
And through these eyes
View the countless lies
Of all those who would know me

Alone with the sun
The clouds dance in fun
There is no more heavenly place
With thousands of hues
In the expanse of blues
Shining upon my face

In this solitude
I cannot be rude
There is no one to dismiss
Just thoughts of guile
And your beautiful smile
With the taunting sweetness of your kiss

Athena

Waves crashing on the jetty rocks
Wind beating my face as I steer toward docks
Against the time of ten thousand clocks
I hold fast my line to harbour beckoning
A thousand plus nights at sea
Searching for Epiphany
Each hard fought battle only pyrrhic victory
As War takes from us everything
Arriving battered from the horizon afar
From a fleet of ship remains we are
Brought home by the North Star
Weathered, torn and laboring

On the shore she appears
Emphatic curves and supple skin
Eyes fierce and glaring as our ship nears
Confidence in a statuesque grin
Wanting only the passage sure
Desire for knowledge of a win not less
Heart overflowing with passion secure
Her need to quench a thirst for success

Determined to endure through the final link
With steady focus on the perilous brink
Perspective hedged on how to think
The War is over but never ended
Solid land offers feelings secure
High seas few dare endure
Wisdom is nigh at the tip of a lure

Life suddenly asks us, are you living as you intended?
Outlasting patience through the endless strokes
Dismissing inveiglement deception provokes
Seduction prevalent with every coax
Our destination never declares coming appended

Easing from the rocky boat
Steady legs don't come quick
Feeling distance in the world remote
At shores edge the senses trick
Her smile beckons us with certain need
Gentleness pervades though concern is bright
Eager touch gives us pause to heed
Loyal are her eyes with light

Settling on the edge of dawn
Ropes secured, knotted and drawn
Crew departed and riggings gone
Left with our thoughts for another board
Uncovering our latest haul
Delivered safely despite storm and squall
Showing for payment against the wall
Another day is scored
With firm hands and hardened back
Lifting tightly and cutting slack
Our winnings sure for award or plaque
Effort is its own reward?

Patience in her soft-toned voice
Direct in her manner and need to connect

Desire fills us to passionately rejoice
To consume her exquisite intellect
Inhaling deep her sumptuous soul
Conflicted from the world afar
My indomitable spirit to shield her whole
Admiring perfection in every scar

Her forceful nature comes with haste
Fixated on success interlaced
Unwavering determination to be embraced
Devotion uncompromised she provides
Valor rises from her heart
Relentless will to deliver equal part
Vigilant imagination and vigor to jumpstart
Her affection victory divides
Tenacity drips from her lips
Captured am I to succumb to her hips
Glamor no paramour can eclipse
Candidly, I resign my fate to her sides

Prowess unmatched for battle ahead
Resilience gleams from her bosom
Sharp wit tipped on her spearhead
She radiates the fortitude of woman

***

Valentine

When our paths first crossed
Your smile pulled me with its brilliant force
Confidence was your spotlight
Then your eyes met mine with magnetic charge
And my world shifted

Where time had been an alibi for
Sleepless nights and unsettled thoughts
My soul is always calmed by the vision of you
Soothing my mind in your mysterious ways
However unsettled

Seconds feel like days between each encounter
When the first words pass your lips
Instantly I am calmed
Excitement takes over my body
Infinite treasure you are to me

There is endless joy in my heart
Having you in my life

I say thank you with every smile

***

Foundation

From the stars you were given to me
Every sunset finds my joy in your mind
Each sunrise brings the sweetness of your kiss
I build every day on your love
Your smile is my bedrock

***

Happiness

Inspiration ignites such fire
Music springing from a lyre
Brilliant light bent from morning dew
Spreading colors in every hue

Lofty clouds bounce up high
Lending contrast for bluest sky
Songs floating gently through the air
Dancing birds without a care

Stars glowing wildly in craving eyes
Bare soul exposed without disguise
Sharing excitement in newest toy
Euphoria ungoverned in pure joy

Softly caressed with silky touch
Enlivened feelings growing much
Captured infinitely in focused stare

Floating exquisitely on the air

In such moments does life awake
Combing thoughts with fierce rake
Igniting the fire of such smiling empress
Gleaming teeth express unbridled happiness

***

A walk under the moon

So bright the night
Walking on sands so white
Crunching stones and crashing waves
Sounding delight in the middle of night

Waves dancing with harvest moon
The wind singing a swinging tune
Alive are shadows all around
Spirits freely moving with night opportune

Around the point to the prominent creek
Darkness desires players who seek
Action bold yet soundly quiet
The moon casts light of glassy mystique

***

Riddle of Love

Millions of ships have been launched in its name
Billions have been healed by its power in prayer

From inside you it comes out
Pumping life into others

More breaths are taken away
Countless hearts are stolen

Everyone falls into it
Few find a way out unscathed

Feeling its energy can overwhelm the timid
Harnessing its power can cure the weak

Through the power of a smile it can end hate
From a look it can inspire progress

Without it humanity could not survive
With it we survive humanity's worst instincts

Tyrants have been dethroned by its simple attack
Turning the other cheek to its attacker

Filled with Understanding, Patience, Acceptance and Forgiveness
Standing beside Faith and Humility

It is our aspiration

Keeping us unbalanced in desperation

Uncontrollable in our addiction to its power
Our bodies powerless to its force

Searching for the meaning in its magic
Comfortable in limbo until it is revealed

Greatness aspires from its grasp
Destruction results from the loss

Attempting to master it with our minds
Submitting to its strength our souls it binds

***

Love remains

All the lies have been forgiven
The silence has been done
Still all my thoughts are driven
Towards your smile glowing like the sun

Alone at night and through morn
Thoughts of you proliferate
Quietly mending this heart well torn
Sweet remembrances do ameliorate

Unable to lose this connection
However severed physically

You pervade my mind in mirror reflection
Becoming my reality

Choice may determine our route
While chance favors the bold
But your lips are still my favorite fruit
In all my stories told

With each breath that I inhaled
Taking rightfully what is mine
You gave to me your soul unveiled
Through eyes joyful as they shine

Now I suffer in my want
Enduring all season and foul weather
Remaining faithful in your taunt
Aware our minds remain together

Unconcerned with all misery of whomever
That should distract your gaze
My desire for you burns forever
And my love remains always

***

The Philosophers Stone

With the power to change all matter to gold
Bringing life to young and old
Stories of its secrets for fortune sold
There is no lightning without thunder

Deep inside hardened walls of protection
Infinite alchemy ignites fires of limitless confection
Pouring new imagination into concoctions of every selection
Time is consumed by metallurgical wonder

Unrelenting in search of alloy exquisite
Mystical enchantment and spiritual realm visit
Passion for thought and creativity requisite
Stubborn determination can no man put asunder

Throughout the ages of our existence
Our aspiration towards the ultimate throne
Pursuing treasure and life eternal with greatest persistence
Revealing the hidden secret of the Philosophers Stone

Catching Victory

PapPap grimaced as he stroked his rough, arthritic hands and flexed his sore, rugged fingers against each other. The sun was merciless in its beating on this hot August day, overpowering everyone in the boat with unbearable heat and not a cloud in the sky to offer some respite from the bright rays. He looked down at the squid on the bait tray thawing from several days in the freezer, taking a long pause on the fishing knife that had been in their family for generations. Slowly, he moved his eyes off the fishing bait and moved them up and over his two grandsons, taking a long pause before he said a word. The world had changed in unfathomable ways since he was their age and he was not about to let this moment go quickly, time held no consequence for these hours with his boys. Life was at a standstill and he was the sole master of the outcome of this day, he was the captain of their universe.

"Throw the anchor, Bud. This is a good spot, let's get started." Pap barked out in his grizzly voice.

Jason quickly pulled the heavy metal anchor out of the front of the bow, untangled the rope and let it over the side of the boat. The anchor splashed and he watched as it disappeared into the deep and followed the rope as it went over until finally there was slack, a sure sign the anchor hit bottom. He turned back to everyone and smiled,

"We're good, it's about twenty feet here. Let's get some fish!"

Derrick looked at Jason and smiled, beginning to take his rod and reel up and undo the hooks from their place in the largest eye on the rod.

"Now just hold on there Deke," Pap started. "Let's make sure we have our rules and everything in order."

Derrick rolled his eyes and started to put his rod back down.

"Sorry Pap, I was just getting ready."

Looking down at the squid, Pap shook his head and took a hard look at Derrick. He grabbed the fishing knife and gripped it hard in his right hand before he began to speak.

"Now, we each have two hooks, and if we start catching fish, there's gonna be a lot of things going on at the same time. So, I'm gonna cut a bunch of bait first. If you think you got one hooked, call it out so we can have the bucket ready. Deke, you are in charge of the bucket, so as the fish go in, you have to make sure there's enough water. You can also bait Jay's hook since he's up front. Are we good?"

Both boys quickly nodded as Pap already went to work on the fish,

"Yes sir!"

Derrick pulled his rod back upright and finished unhooking the line, feeling the tension of the line slack as he leaned the rod over the side of the boat.

More spectacular days for fishing could not be found on the Long Island Sound or anyplace in the world for that matter, at this time of year, with these particular fishermen in the boat. Eight states and 700 miles often separated all three of them during the normal course of life, but on this fortunate occasion they were all together in the most intimate surrounding of the vast Long Island Sound under their twelve foot aluminum fishing boat with a bright sun shining, no wind in the air, not a ripple on the placid, glass-like water and a perfect tide to support their efforts. The quiet solitude between them was not distance, but a unique communication that expressed their deep affection for each other. In the calm of the silence, everything necessary that words try to convey was communicated with an acute sense of appreciation for the high-level of thought and deep understanding that each of them had for this moment.

"Here fishy, fishy," Deke started. "C'mover here fishy, fishy."

Pap went about cutting the bait while Deke continued to call gently to the water and the fish below.

"Hello fish," Jay began, "I got this nice piece of bait on these hooks for you and I want you to just take a nibble at it. Just try a small bite. I am sure you will like it. Just nibble, that's all I need you to do, just nibble."

Pap kept his head down so the boys could not see his proud smile. He had told them that the secret to fishing was talking to the fish, and they were going about it with great enthusiasm. He couldn't hold back a chuckle as he listened to the call and response between Deke and Jay that was almost in syncopated rhythm, as they spoke to the fish after each other.

"What's so funny Pap?" Deke asked.

"Besides your face?" Pap smiled back.

Jay let out a roar as the boat started to rock from his laughter. Deke sucked his teeth and smiled.

"Man, I was just trying to talk to the fish, why you getting on me?"

Pap chuckled again. "Deke, I'm just getting a kick outta the way you're talking to the fish. DO you talk to girls the same way?"

Jay let out a second roar and the boat rocked again. Deke laughed.

"Well, only if it works."

Pap laughed hard and started coughing. He had trouble catching his breath as he tried to fight between the laughing and wheezing. Deke and Jay suddenly looked concerned as Pap continued to fight for his breath.

"I'm alright, I'm alright," Pap continued.

He hocked up a huge ball of phlegm and spit into the water. Slowly they all returned to the tips of their rods and the line stringing into the deep water below.

"I got one!" Jay yelled as he pulled his rod high into the air and started reeling in with a fury. The boat rocked dramatically as Jay pulled his rod back and both Pap and Deke had to grab onto the rail to steady themselves.

"Dangit Jay, easy with your rod, don't go throwing us all out of the boat!" Pap shouted.

"Hey! I got one too!" Derrick shouted and began to reel in his line fast with excitement.

"Easy boys," Pap began, "this is only the beginning of the day, and you'll pull the line right out of the fish and scare'em away. Take your time."

No sooner did Pap speak when his line started to pull and he realized that he had a fish on his line too.

"Hey, Hey! Deke get that bucket ready, looks like we are all bringing in dinner."

For the better part of the next 90 minutes, the aluminum boat was a fluid process of chaos in artistry as the syncopated rythyms of reels mixed with splashes, thuds and shrieks of excitement. PapPap could barely keep still as he continued to cut pieces of squid while his own line pulled from fish nibbling on his hooks. Derrick and Jason were pulling up porgies two at a time in lock step with each other as they quickly re-baited and dropped their lines. As the bucket began to overflow with the catches of the day, Derrick suddenly realized there was no more room for fish.

"Pap? The bucket's full and there's no room for more water, what do we do?" Derrick asked confused.

"Just throw 'em in the back of the boat with me, boys, we got a school under us and we've got plenty of day left."

Continuing at a blistering pace, the boat began to overload with fish. Fins were flittering and fish were flopping all over the place and laughter filled the air as the three fishermen realized they were out of room to take in anymore. "Alright, I think we've taken in our fill for today boys." Pap finally bellowed in his gruff voice. Derrick and Jason looked at each other with knowing smiles and began to tighten up their rods and reels and get the boat ready for the ride home. Jason handed his rod to Derrick to put on the side of the seat and turned quickly to pull up the anchor. The routine was an unspoken one that was quickly dispatched in action and finished with each passenger putting their life seat comfortably under them as Pap turned and pulled the string on the motor.

The motor roared on the first pull, a sure sign of a great day and captured all of their excitement as they realized home was just a short journey away. PapPap clicked the Johnson nine-point-nine engine into forward and revved it firmly, thrusting the small boat powerfully through the glassy water. Jason looked down over the side of the boat to see his reflection and look for any jellyfish, a sure sign that summer was ending soon. Derrick looked at PapPap and then beyond him toward Connecticut and slowly wondered if this could be the way every summer ended.

When they arrived home, Jeanne was waiting on the beach with Pepper and a thrilling smile. She knew the boys had to have a great day to have been out so long. Jason jumped out of the boat first, pulled the nose onto the beach securely and then ran up to Jeanne who was holding the roller for the boat to be rolled up the beach.

"How many did you catch, buddy?" Jeanne smiled.

"Mom, the whole boat is full of fish. Take a look."

Jeanne walked slowly up to the boat and started laughing. PapPap and Derrick started laughing too.

"I'm not cleaning any of these fish!" She started.

"No Aunt Jeanne, we're gonna clean them." Derrick replied.

The boys worked quickly with PapPap and Jeanne to get the boat up the beach to the house and secure it for the night. Then they began the long, arduous process of gutting and scaling the fish, getting them ready for PapPap's famous fishcakes. On the outside deck, the hose was spraying, buckets were filled with guts and laughter was heard as the two young boys went about the business of cleaning the fish. An activity that should take the better part of thirty minutes with an efficient fisherman was bound to take the better part of an hour as the two young fishermen recounted their memories of the day, who had the biggest fish and which fish fought the hardest.

PapPap finished washing up in the kitchen and put on the kettle while he waited for the boys to finish their work cleaning.

"That was some day you boys had out there." Jeanne began.

"Yup." Pap replied.

"Most you ever caught, Dad?" Jeanne continued.

"Well, I don't know, but I think it's the most fun I ever had." PapPap laughed.

Jeanne smiled in admiration of her father's joy but also his stoicism in the face of all the challenges life continued to throw at him. The kettle boiled and whistled and slowly, Pap turned down the burner, grabbing the kettle and pouring the hot water into his mug and teabag. Picking up the steeping tea, he walked carefully across the redwood floorboards as they creaked an evening tune and moved slowly to the large picture windows that looked out on the expanse of the beach and the deck where the boys were playing and finishing their cleanup of the day's catch. Unbeknownst to themselves, the boys suddenly took pause from their play and turned carefully towards the window where PapPap stood looking out on the water and to the horizon beyond and without hesitation all three of the fishermen looked at each other and smiled knowingly.

    The orange sun was setting over a lowering tide and the sky was a million hues of purple, blue, and gold that seemed to burst off of every cloud in the sky. As he brought the mug to his lips with a satisfaction for the day's events, PapPap took a deep breath and held it closely in his chest. Then he let out a long deep sigh, exhaling the challenges of his aging body and oncoming illness all at once. There, in that moment, on that picture-perfect evening, after that spectacular day of fishing with his boys, PapPap accepted the fate of his existence once and for all. He had conquered this great day with total victory, perhaps his greatest, understanding fully that it may never happen again for him with the time he had left on this earth. He smiled without regret at that promise.

SAND

Our toughest moments are often remembered not for the painful experience, but our survival from that pain and our willingness to continue on and endure more. Sand is the grit that gets into everything. It represents the incredible power of nature that grinds away at our skin and tears at the fabric of everything, leaving us raw and exposed. Sand attracts us with its soft appearance, but then scours everything when the wind picks it up, or the ocean churns in a storm. It is tough, taking the constant beating of the ocean waves throughout time, recording all of our history and stories. As Heraclitus wrote, "History is a child building a sand-castle by the sea, and that child is the whole majesty of man's power in the world."

The Crown

Under the weight that burdens me
Heavy as the mountain which I stand
I mind the world beneath me
Moving forward at my command

Protector of its darkest secrets
Whispered quiet in latest hours
Action demanded for failed agreements
The consequence of violated powers

Though I stand with tremendous might
Showing strength beyond compare
Wisdom is my greatest light
Inhaling patience for fresh air

Veracity defends my greatest slip
Made with certainty of choice
As captain must I steer this ship
To the heavens shall I rejoice

Looming enemies are always near
Ever caustic and primed for fight
Stalking fast each new frontier
Must we crush them from our sight

Seldom does joy come to call
Lest a ruler regales his clown
It is the sovereign who bears it all
In solitude uneasy wears the crown

Torture

Did you scream
As you severed the connection between us
Or did you savor the sensation of pain
Burning deep in your mind

Were your eyes dry with conviction
As you took action
Or do tears still flow freely
Keeping you comfort in your misery

How did you pierce the heart
So cold and callous
Was it pleasure to feel the penetration
As you struck me deep inside

What did you feel in your soul
When you saw my reaction
Where was your mind
Watching me writhe in anguish

Is it pleasing to your ears
Hearing my cries for your return to me
Does the hurt in my voice
Thrill you in delight

Was it easy to erase
The image of my face
Or do you suffer willingly
With the absence in my place

Naked Arms

Standing patiently in the shadows
There remains discomfort
Subtle in the unkempt corners
Reminding upon observation that care is always necessary

Letting go of control
Selfish emotions
Allowing a greater sense of purpose to fill the void
Keeping the shadow at ease

There are no ghosts to conquer
No spirits to vanquish
There is just the empty space
Only silence will listen to your thoughts

Searching the confines of the mind to find peace
Random thoughts ravage the timid soul
Sturdiness comes through determination
Confidence with forthright action

Belief keeps the spirit fresh
Growing exuberant as the senses
Purpose lives in positive thoughts
Plying the tendrils of Faith as it strengthens with every small gain

Distance does not exist in the shadows
Nor does time

There is only the imagination
Ideas of what can exist

Tired and heavy arms
Naked in the abyss of dark
Hoping to be filled soon
My chest of love awaits you

***

The pulchritude of a tumultuous cryptic enigma called my mind

From my eyes can I see a world far smaller than my imagination
Kids playing stickball on city streets
Boats speeding across calm waters
Seagulls dropping mussels on the rocky beach
Soccer games of incredible skill in the park

My mind drifts willingly to sudden chirping in the distance
A butterfly lands on a nearby blade of grass
There is no kite flying today, but it is a perfect day for a kite
Even the bluest sky is lonely without a cloud
Crickets in the evening keep us feeling safe and not alone

Saying hello to a stranger is not advised, but it is not forbidden
We never know who will be the one to brighten our day
Courtesy never hurts and often helps us in tough times

***

Snow drifts

Snow falling
In my head drifts
The wisping white meadows
Of unclouded flakes
Floating seamlessly
carried with the wind
Blows harshly
As the frosted droplets
Rest in white
Uneasy are the footprints

***

Trees without leaves

February is such a bland month
Always so cold
Bleak best describes the days
No one wants to go out at nights

The sun is not as low in the sky
But it is not much higher
The days are slow to get longer
Though they are not as short

Shadows in the second month
are longer in the height of day
The appearance that it is later
than it really is

On snowy days the park is empty
An occasional exception may jog by
With great effort
Leaving their impact with big footprints

On sunny days squirrels and birds bustle
Hustling to get their activities in order
For the year ahead
There is little time to waste on a good day

There amongst the signs of life
Long shadows are cast by the trees
Their branches are somewhat diffused
As they stand there without leaves

Death of a Child

Your arrival came with greatest joy delivered
How sweet a face even blindest eye adores
Into the cold world your body shivered
Shrieking like burning embers in your pores

Beauty has no equal in such visage
Resting with such peaceful countenance
Born from silkiest threads of woven dreams montage
Wildest imagination mesmerizing thoughts to dance

Inspiration for you given from the sweetest love
Conceived in our minds with greatest joy
Glorious hues of ecstasy floating high above
Consideration without care for girl or boy

Our connection bore the luscious fruit of your soul
Bonding our hearts and minds in total purpose
Magnificent the idea of you melding is whole
Infinitely deep bore thoughts of you below the surface

Now inconsolable I lie despondent
My faith tested by such depths of sorrow tasted
Absent of my hopes and actions confident
Feeling dark and sour with cause wasted

Lifeless rests this angel in my mind

The sweetest vision of such love eternal
Lost from all embrace through actions unkind
Burning my soul on fire with hate infernal

***

Grief

It comes in waves and all at once
Pounding down upon the shore
Beating rocks
Beating sand
Beating my body sore

Crashing onto jetties
Sending sea spray everywhere
Feel of drops
Or teardrops
Feeding my despair

Under gray clouds of loneliness
Hours past the break of dawn
You come to me
Suddenly
Stopped from moving on

In your eyes I see the stars
Your smile is glowing bright
How I miss you
Might I kiss you

Hug you with all my might

In the wind exists a howl
Stealing my remembrance brief
Like cold December
I will remember
Rejoicing you overcomes my grief

***

Atlas humbled

While time weighs heavy in patient arms
My reassurance not expected
Though exposed, concern is not of harms
Faith brings strength in thoughts collected

That my burden seem enormous extent
These broad shoulders were built for more
With fortitude to carry all discontent
Courage endures forevermore

Yet my devotion be not for want
Deafening silence in your response
Alone I gather endless taunt
Captured cold in chilling nonchalance

For every breath I feel your pain
Beguiling anguish and such blue
Concealed my motive not in vain

This abject load I bear for you

Though I remain steadfast and willing
in absence of my relief
I kneel humbled
until my final breath be thief

***

The Burden of lies

Your words fester like a pile of rotting sushi
Climbing a broken ladder held together by one rung
Acrimonious are the dregs of putrid wine swallowed
Fetid stories wafting in the air from such vile tongue

Convincing in your rancor of false promise
Serving moldy confection and sour canapés
Nothing solid or sure in your foundation
Where truth should remain only disappointment stays

Now surrounds you a crumbled wall of deception
Casting consternation of loathsome looks in shameful eyes
Where savored trust and valued loyalty should taste sweet

Remains such stench so sultry from the burden of your lies

Heavy anchor holds fast your sinking ship
Drowning in the sea of prevarication
Where freedom from such weight requires admission
Silence bans the heart from such elation

Crushing is the gravity of truth
Yet light and free is the feeling of its embrace
There is no cost for submitting to its power
Such humility will release your shame, guilt and disgrace

***

So in love

So in love are you
My head is bloody from your beatings
Black and blue bruises show your passion
You care so much that blood spills freely

So in love are you
The deafness has overcome my ears
Screams directed by your innermost concerns for my safety
Whatever I said was wrong I misheard you

So in love are you
Spending time with friends is too much
It would take away from our special time
And you need to be greedy with me alone

So in love are you
Family chooses to stay away
They lack the understanding for what we have
And what we have is too powerful for family

So in love are you
Our pets must live outside
There is no room in the house for distraction
And I should have cleaned up that mess

So in love are you
Babies should not be crying
Tears only soil the sweet moments that make them
Their diapers are supposed to carry that mess

So in love are you
I do not need to make a living
Bills cannot interfere with the heat of our desire
You will figure out how we need to survive

So in love are you

***

Black Consideration

He's too thoughtful
That's not it
He's too forgiving
No.
He's too understanding
Why can't I describe this
He's too willing
This is complicated
He's too overbearing
No. That's not right at all
He's too involved
I can't believe this is so difficult
He's too attentive
Can that really be possible?
He's too inquisitive
Why did I even say that?
He's overwhelming
Is that really what he is?
Or am I just overwhelmed by what he is doing to me?
What is he doing to me?
Why can't I get control of myself around him?
Where did I lose my ability to think?
I don't remember anyone ever being so considerate
Is that what it is?
Yes.
How can anyone be so ......?
It's just not natural

It's freakish
He's too considerate

Vacation Nightmare

Moist hands touched Shaunelle's sensitive neck as she began to settle back into her large first-class seat on the overcrowded plane. Suddenly, she realized these soft, wet hands touching her were her own, she had been thinking about Caleb again and had gotten lost in the idea of him touching her, making her feel uncomfortably sublime. Just having texted him goodbye until she reached her homeland of Jamaica, her mind had drifted to their first passionate kiss weeks before on the Nautical Mile and then to their night together the day before. His piercing blue eyes radiated through her and left her bare and exposed to his imagination. Caleb was tall, six foot something, with an imposing stance and incredibly soft, gentle hands that made her feel alive when he touched her. Introduced to a universe of ecstasy she had never known before, he was educating her in a world of pleasure that seemed surreal and impossible to imagine, leaving her perplexed as to why none of her previous lovers had ever been able to bring her a tenth of the way to this incredible place in her mind.

Startling her from the intimate memory, the cold, nasally voice began,

"Do you fly much to Jamaica? Or is this your first time?"

The gentleman seated next to her began. Large and corpulent with a receding hairline, his pasty skin and a sense of fashion from nineteen sixty-three was appaling. Shaunelle slowly turned to her neighbor and started with a confused look,

"I'm sorry, I'm not really in the mood for talking, but yes, I am from Jamaica if that is what you were asking."

Her neighbor's smile didn't flinch an ounce at the sound of Shaunelle's words as he continued boldly to engage her in the one-sided conversation,

"Well that's great to hear! You don't sound Jamaican, though. My name is Phil and this is my first time to Jamaica. I'm going down there at the invitation of the Minister of Finance, he and I played golf earlier this year in a charity tournament and he told me he would be happy to host me if I ever decided to come visit. So, I took him up on the offer since I have some vacation time and it seems like a great place to visit."

Shaunelle began to look into her purse for her iPhone and put the headphones in her ears.

"That's nice." She turned quickly towards Phil.

Quickly texting Caleb in hopes he could give her some advice, she tried to act as if she was going to listen to music. Phil continued undeterred,

"So where are you from on the island? Are you going back to see your family? What do you recommend I should see while I am down there?"

Caleb wasn't responding to her text and Shaunelle was beginning to feel the anxiety in her chest, she didn't want to have to tell Phil to shut up, but she was beginning to lose it. Finally, Caleb responded with the witty remark she needed to distance herself from Phil and everything around her.

"Just listen to the songs I sent you. Can you hear Bob singing "Every little thing, is gonna be alright...." He texted.

She smiled and let out a deep breath knowing that everything was going to be ok as long as she had Caleb in her life. Her smile was too wide to conceal as Phil began to start talking again, but Shaunelle turned on Caleb's song and turned away towards the window, she wanted to be lost in her thoughts of Caleb as the plane began its takeoff.

Startling her from her sleep, Shaunelle woke dazed, confused and annoyed at Phil's grabbing and shaking her. She was about to scream on him when she suddenly realized it was not Phil but her ex-boyfriend, Gerald, sitting next to her in Phil's seat. She gave him a cold, hard look and then remembered that he was on this flight with eight of their other friends. She wasn't happy about him being there, but there was not much she could control about the situation.

"What do you want Gerald?" she started.

Gerald looked her up and down and paused, he wanted to make sure he had her attention before he began.

"Shaunelle, you know I realize things between us are not the way we wanted them to be," he started, "I hear you have a new boyfriend now?" Gerald probed in his usual arrogant manner.

Shaunelle couldn't believe the audacity of this man in front of her, who had broken her heart one too many times.

"Gerald, stop it. You have no right to ask me about my boyfriend. What are you doing here anyway? Why are you even on this trip?" Shaunelle blurted out with more certainty than she expected.

Suddenly she was taken aback by her own courage.

"I'm sorry. What do you want Gerald?" She continued.

Gerald was stunned by her show of confidence and questioning of him. He was expecting her submissive to reveal itself far more easily, yet here she was, showing a standoffish position that was neither usual or comforting.

"I want you back Shaunelle, and I am willing to do whatever it takes. I'm not going to leave Jamaica without your hand in marriage." Gerald said boldly, trying to take back control of the situation.

Shaunelle put her headphones back in her ears and rolled her eyes as she began to turn away from Gerald.

"Goodbye Gerald. Don't speak to me again for this entire trip. I really don't want to talk to you and I don't want to hear anything like this again from you. Just leave me alone."

Shaunelle tried to go back to sleep while Gerald sat there in Phil's seat beside her, staring in disbelief. She could feel him burning a hole in her even with her eyes closed. But she wasn't about to give in to him and she was beginning to dread the next two weeks.

Startled from her sleep, Shaunelle turned her head to see Phil smiling at her.

"You mustav been really tired! You didn't move from your position since I got back in my seat." Phil chuckled.

Painfully, Shaunelle felt the crick in her neck and realized her predicament. She had been tired and was dreaming about her incredible encounter with Caleb the day before, he had worn her out physically and mentally with a sexual energy she never encountered. Then she had stayed up all night packing to get on this flight. She rubbed her neck as she looked at Phil and realized they had safely landed in Montego Bay. She grimaced as she realized this trip was not what as she had originally planned.

The cool breeze felt good as it touched the back of Shaunelle's neck, raising goosebumps slightly, as she gazed out on the blue water of the Caribbean Sea. Sitting among the group of ten friends, eating fish and festival, drinking Red Stripe's and laughing at stories of younger days and smiling, she wished this moment could last forever. Looking down at her phone, she smiled as she saw a text from Caleb and quickly replied,

"I wish you were here."

"He must really be something special" Darren leaned over and whispered.

Shaunelle nodded without looking up.

"He is something really special. He always knows exactly what to say, do, think, touch - he's in my mind constantly in a good way. I've never felt this way about anyone."

"Yeah, that pretty obvious." Darren chuckled. "You haven't spent two minutes without looking at your phone. You're sprung."

Shaunelle punched Darren playfully in the arm and he reacted,

"Ow, Damn girl, why you hit me? I'm just saying the truth!" They both smiled and laughed.

"So, is it really serious?" Darren continued.

"Yes, it is. I can't imagine life without him. He means the world to me. He's the first man who gets me, and he is so amazing the way he looks at everything and considers things. And he's incredible in bed too. It's scary."

Darren was shocked by Shaunelle's forthright comment.

"Damn girl! You don't need to brag now, I didn't ask you all that!"

Everyone turned their head at his comment and suddenly they realized they were not alone. Shaunelle blushed quickly as she realized she had been cavalier with her words, but she did not regret saying anything. Darren let out a laugh to lighten the mood, and everyone went back to their conversation, both of them quietly acknowledging the discomfort.

Unpacking her bags in her room, a hesitant knock on the door turned Shaunelle's head slightly from the decision she was trying to make for the evenings footwear - pumps or flats was never an easy decision in the company of this group, which was always trying to look too cute and about the baller lifestyle, even if they were all really broke in reality.

"What is it?" She asked in the direction of the door.

"May I come in?" the voice quietly replied.

She realized it was Darren, but it wasn't his normal voice, he seemed hesitant, concerned.

"Come in Darren, what's wrong?" Shaunelle went back to unpacking her shoes and hesitating on her own decision for her outfit.

"Do you think I should go with these pumps with this outfit, or these flats with this outfit?" Shaunelle asked to break the awkward silence.

She and Darren had been friends for nearly ten years and she trusted his fashion sense, if nothing else she could always rely on him for helping her with these decisions.

"Go with the pumps tonight. I know you're not in the mood, but you don't want to draw the wrong attention to yourself. Go with the flow. Everyone is looking Gucci tonight, you might as well touch'em with a little something." Darren replied.

Shaunelle knew he was right even though she didn't want to wear the pumps. She was tired and more than anything wanted to stay in bed and just FaceTime with Caleb, but she knew she wasn't going to get out of the event this evening with everyone.

"Ugh, I knew you were going to say that," she began, then realized Darren was really hiding something,

"Darren, what are you not telling me? What's wrong?"

Darren looked at her bags and then out the window at the fading light in the horizon past the sea,

"You know me, Shaunelle, I don't try to get in the middle of anyone's business. But-" Shaunelle cut him off,

"But what, Darren? Spit it out!"

Darren blinked and shook his head, then brought his eyes to hers and continued,

"Look, you know why Gerald is here, and he's serious, he's not taking no for an answer. I know you got this new guy and you're into him, I get it, but Gerald is here-"

"I know Gerald is here Darren! But we're DONE and that's it! I'm not ever going back there. And I don't fucking appreciate the lecture!" Shaunelle snapped.

"No Shaunelle, I'm sorry, I'm not trying to lecture, I'm trying to ask what I should do to help you. You're my friend and Gerald is my friend, but this is awkward and I don't know what to do."

Shaunelle sighed. "What do you mean Darren? There is nothing to do. We're on vacation and I just have to deal with the fact that Gerald's arrogant ass is here and he's just going to fucking annoy me until we leave. I'm trying not to think about it. It puts me in a really bad mood."

Darren nodded, "You know he thinks he's going to get you to say yes before this trip is over, right?"

Shaunelle laughed, "Then he's really stupid, which we already knew. Darren, why would I ever go back to someone who hit me and cheated on me? Gerald is an asshole! You're friends with an asshole! Why am I even discussing this with you?"

Darren frowned. "I know he's an asshole, but we've been boys for life. But you're my friend too. Tell me how you want to handle it and I will not let him bother you for the trip."

Shaunelle looked Darren straight in the eye and paused for a deep breath. She realized Darren was not here to confront her, he was afraid that she would lose her cool with Gerald and do something insane that might embarrass all of them in public or worse, land them all in jail.

"You're not here because you want to help me. You're here because the others put you up to this, they want to know if you think I might freak out or go crazy tonight if Gerald tries to push up on me or something. You just need to know if I'm gonna keep it together. Well the answer is yes, I'm gonna keep it together, in fact, I'm gonna make Gerald fucking jealous as hell and you should be worrying about his stupid ass, you fucking moron! Now get the fuck out of here before I start screaming on your ass!"

Darren was paralyzed by Shaunelle's response. She sliced through him with her tongue and there was no real reaction to have, except to leave. He paused before turning to exit, then looked back at her glaring eyes and smiled wryly at her.

"Alright girl, we gonna have fun tonight."

Shaunelle snapped back, "Get your stupid ass out of my face."

As Darren closed the door behind him, she finally let a smile overcome her face and grabbed the phone to text Caleb.

The morning glare of sunlight on the beach didn't bode well for Shaunelle's hangover. Events from the night's outing were still foggy in her head, but she did not feel good at all about what may have transpired. She was hoping it was all a nightmare, she would wake up in Caleb's arms laughing and smiling at him, but the silence coming from the Beach house was a sign that things were not going to start well this morning.

"You ok girl?" Teodora asked.

Shaunelle didn't hear her come from the house on the soft sand as she sat down in the chaise next to Shaunelle.

"I just have a bad headache, I think it's just exhaustion." Shaunelle began.

"Girl, who you telling? I don't know how you got away from Gerald when his ass was chasing you all night around the clubs." Teodora continued.

Shaunelle couldn't respond. Her heart sank as she began to revisit the past 12 hours. Gerald had been relentless in his pursuit of her, and with every drink he consumed he got bolder and more reckless. Her hazy recollection of events was beginning to clear enough for her to remember that he had stormed into her room at the end of the night and tried to force himself on her. Darren and Trevon had to pull him away as she was kicking and screaming.

"Where is Darren?" Shaunelle asked.

Teodora paused knowing the answer would only set Shaunelle off. "Oh, you know girl, he took Gerald into town to blow some steam. He called me and said they were gonna go rent some jet skis and stay out on the water for the morning."

Shaunelle was silent. She didn't know whether to laugh or scream but her head was pounding and she needed to get away from everyone. Shaunelle got up and walked into the house.

"I'm going to make some breakfast, do you want anything?" Shaunelle began.

"No girl, I'm good." Teodora replied.

"Can you come to Jamaica if I buy you a ticket?" Shaunelle texted Caleb.

He wasn't replying fast enough for her. "I need you here really bad." She continued.

"Sure. That's really expensive Babe, but if you need me. When were you thinking?" Caleb replied.

"Today." Shaunelle answered.

The pause was excruciating for Shaunelle. She needed Caleb desperately.

"Babe, you know that's impossible. Your best chance is a flight tomorrow if you can book a fare."

Shaunelle slowly relaxed after Caleb brought her gently back to Earth. He always talked the sense into her that she needed. She went into the kitchen and opened the refrigerator to find the ingredients for an omlette. Her hangover was raging and no ordinary eggs would due. She pulled out some peppers, onions, spinach, cheese and bacon with the eggs and quickly began to whisk her way into a hearty breakfast that she needed to feast on after all the drama of the past 24 hours.

The morning sun was high in the late May sky when Gerald and Darren zoomed up to the beach house in their jetskis. Teodora screamed as Gerald whirred around and sprayed her soaking wet from the exhaust of his propeller.

"You fucking asshole! What de hell wrong wit ya stupid ass!" Teodora yelled.

Shaunelle peered out the doorway to see Darren laughing at Teodora, who was screaming at both of them furiously. Shaunelle rolled her eyes and walked back into her room.

"You want to ride the jetski?" Darren asked Shaunelle.

"Sure. Can you show me how?" Shaunelle replied.

Darren waited as Shaunelle closed her book and grabbed her sunglasses. Her bikini bathing suit held her perfectly as the two walked out onto the beach. Everyone was in the water on jetskis. Shaunelle glared at Gerald who was starring impatiently in their direction, but he quickly looked away when she grimaced harder.

"Here, the starter is on your left hand and the throttle is on your right. When you start it, it will be in drive, so all you have to do is push the throttle and go. Make sure you hold on tight." Darren explained.

"Okay, so what if it runs out of gas?" Shaunelle asked.

Darren laughed, "No Shaunelle, for this to run out of gas you have to be out there all day."

Shaunelle hopped on the jetski, hit the start button and pressed the throttle, zooming forward before Darren could say anything else.

Flying through the water, Shaunelle was finally free. She had been regretting taking this trip and was missing Caleb terribly, but the jetski was clearing out the stress and aggravation of the last 24 hours. She roared around the shoreline and raced out into the middle of the ocean, hoping to run out of gas and be stuck far out a sea away from everyone. Slowly, as the frustrations disapated, Shaunelle turned the jetski around and decided to return back to the beach where the people looked like ants were on the horizon.

The roar of jetskis overwhelmed Shaunelle as Darren and Gerald pulled up beside her. Suddenly she was racing these two idiots and felt somewhat out of control, but she wasn't going to let them intimidate her. She pressed the throttle hard and opened up the engine full, taking off in front of them. She laughed as she looked back at their distorted faces. Gerald was not at all happy and throttled his jetski forward. He was too close and Shaunelle started to lose balance. Just then Darren roared across Shaunelle path and her jetski clipped his and swerved wildly out of control. Shaunelle was all at once in the air and heading towards a jetty of big rocks. The jetski splashed into the water and hurtled Shaunelle forward into the rocks, knocking her unconscious.

The light glared as Shaunelle slowly woke. Her head was pounding and her whole body was in pain. As she started to gather her surroundings, she began to make out faces and voices.

"Where am I?" Shaunelle began.

"Oh, Shaunelle baby, you're gonna be ok."

Shaunelle recognized the voice, it was her mothers'.

"Mom? What happened?" Shaunelle asked.

"Hmm. Well from what Gerald told me, you were lucky. You could have been killed. What were you thinking going so fast on that jet thing?"

Shaunelle was confused. She couldn't remember what happened and didn't understand what was going on.

"Mommy? Where am I? What's going on?" Shaunelle cried.

"You hit your head and broke your leg baby. Don't worry, everything is going to be ok." Shaunelle's mother continued.

"Where's Caleb? I need to see Caleb?" Shaunelle started to sob.

"Who's Caleb? You mean Gerald? He's coming baby. He just went to take care of a few things for you, now that you're engaged."

Shaunelle felt the panic in her chest.

"Engaged? What do you mean, engaged? Engaged who? Mommy I just met Caleb, we've only been dating a few weeks."

Shaunelle's mother looked confused.

"Baby, you just hit your head. Gerald told me you accepted his proposal this morning. There's no Caleb, that's just your imagination."

Shaunelle slowly looked down at her left hand and began to cry as she saw the diamond ring sparkling on her finger. Her heart was beating uncontrollably fast and her hands were sweating profusely, as she suddenly realized she was lost, alone, and without her phone.

SALT

Passion is the essence of the human spirit. What drives us to achieve great accomplishments and surpass our own expectations is the desire to be more than what we see ourselves to be in the mirror. Salt is the passion that is the spice of life. It brings out the flavor of our experiences and enhances our senses to the mustiness of the erotic and esoteric. How we are able to pursue dreams and fantasies, capture hearts and win minds is all about leaving a residue with the people we touch. On the beach, salt is in the air and makes it smell different. It is in the water and is corrosive to anything metal, rusting even to most hardened alloys. Salt gets into our clothes, our furniture, our hair with a stickiness that is never easy to come out. As Georg Wilhelm Fredric Hegel said, "Nothing great in the world has ever been accomplished without passion."

Heavenly Bonds

The shock of sudden locking eyes
Feelings can no words disguise
From the heart a revealing clue
Fastened secure without compromise

Elevation toward higher view
Enlightened thoughts and ideas new
Through passion and synergy comes
Unfettered energy coursing true

Bodies joined as each succumbs
Fired hearts beating battle drums
Tying together with heavenly bonds
Full release sacred knowledge becomes

***

Your Mind

Sunsets encapsulate the infinite beauty of the mind at work
Filled with ideas and thoughts in every hue and color
Light bouncing off clouds and water with even greater contrast
Magnificence of the setting sun framed by horizon between heaven and earth

Each sunset tells a different, unique story about that day
How every challenge arose and the small moments in between
Highlights, if there were any, stand out with brighter tint
Low points are faded into the background so no noticeable flaw is apparent

Each sunset feels like I am intimate with your mind
Wrapped in the passion of imagining your thoughts
Slowly unravelling the nerves and feelings bundled together inside of you
Undressing your emotions until they lay as bare as your body in front of me

Your naked mind exposed is breathtaking
Simple in its desire to fulfill my needs, body, mind and soul
Complex in its plans to carry out such goals
Mysterious with its responses to receipt of each step taken

Penetrating your mind is exhilarating with each stroke
Slowly probing your walls until they soften and come down
Allowing me to explore your deepest regions with ease
Passion rising in me to know every detail of your thought process

Connecting with your mind is celestial
Synapses firing at the speed of light between our thoughts
Fire spreading throughout our bodies as our minds fill each other with pleasure
Shockwaves of delight overtake us as full connection is maintained

Flying through the skies as our minds meld together
Unison in our rhythmic thinking with each breath
Feelings flowing from every pore of our being
Tremendous heat building from our increasing rate of process
Holding back from the process ending
Our minds fighting our bodies for control
Ecstasy knocking at the door with increasing volume
Steady waves of elation begin to crash over each other, again and again

Begging for permission to give in
Your voice betrays you at last
you plead, please
You mind knows it can no longer withhold

Overflowing, you consume me
Exploding from somewhere deep inside
I can no longer withstand your grasp
Draining in total eruption

Overtaken by uncontrollable smiles
Showering cooling thoughts
Embrace keeping our connection firm
Basking in the sunset of our minds together

***

Want

You come for me in the moments haunting
Before light breaks the shroud of dark
Exhaling with a moan so taunting
The coldest eyes ignite in spark

Torment floats above your voice
Shudders stabbing thickly through the air
Halting pitches leaving little choice
What direction must we dare

Inhaling deeply all your scent
Extending the stretch of my sphere
Not a second to be careless spent
Exploring all this new frontier

Invigorated from a gentle touch
Of lips upon smooth thighs
Gathering softly in as much
The passion in your eyes

Gasping quickly in your throat

All that is left to aspire
Unleashing the river of wildest connote
Running rampant with desire

Violent torture is all that keeps
Darkness from shedding its cloak
Thick and moist of salt and weeps
Captured firmly in each stroke

Imminent with convulsions present
Engorged with lust the senses increase
Reaching peak after peak of the highest assent
No mercy being granted full release

***

Missing You

Do you still gasp
When you think of my kiss
How I steal your breath away

Are my hands still soft
As you gently hold them
While yours grow moist with excitement

Do you still listen
For the beat of my heart
Resting your head on my chest

The sound of your voice pervades my soul
The touch of your fingers raises my skin
Looking into your eyes
I search for heaven deep within

Tasting your love
Knowing its scent
It's all that consumes me
Leaving me in desperate want

Each gentle kiss
Every subtle touch
Hearing the shortness in your breath
Sensing your need

Stroking your thighs
While we let others watch
Your smile radiating
At the enthusiasm of my touch

The light of your smile overwhelms my heart
Your gaze upon me warm
Feeling the love inside you
Riding together through the storm

Consuming your mouth
In quiet veracity
Your tongue my slave
Willing to my determination

In every small riddle

Teasing your mind
Keeping your interest
Enjoying each response
Do you miss my presence with my absence
Are tears common to your night
Do you feel me missing you
Wanting to make everything right

***

Possession

Inhaling your lingering scent
Remnants of the memory of you being here with me
Unbridled love fragrant in the air
Released from every pore
Strengthening the bonds that grow between us

Inside your mind is where I belong
Feeling deep into the darkest parts of your thoughts
Tearing down your walls
Finding you
Bare, Naked, Afraid, Alone

Strong and warm I embrace you
Protecting you in my love
Bringing you out from the darkness
Sharing your light with the world

Exposing guilt and shame to fresh air
where they cannot live

Sharing my mind with yours
Listening to the beat of my heart
Capturing your fear with my arms
Keeping your hands safe on my chest
Igniting the fire deep inside your heart

Our connection grows stronger
Fire burning in excitement
Energy raging between us
Consuming time and space all around
Endless in its hunger for our passion

Nothing can quench its thirst
Overwhelming any resistance to its surge
Tightening its grip on unconditional love
Erupting with celestial force
Grasping your full love in total possession

***

Wet

Each word imprints on her mind
Leaving in its place a slightly damp experience
Not aware of the sudden change her body has made

Similar to a shift from high to low pressure fronts
Moisture is certain in the air
Showers are due at any time

Certain triggers cause this spontaneous burst of liquid
Flowing freely as it arrives
Thick and musty with purpose

Delivering an exquisite sense of passion
Intoxicating the senses
Flooding everything in its wake

Heavy fluid transforms simple breathing into complex vocal sounds
Her movements ease into convulsions
Shaking ankles and knees lead the way for tremendous overload

Increasing rates of blood pumping and viscous textures produce
Rising levels of heat
Beads of sweat engage deliberate droplets of brackish delight

She is swimming in ecstasy
Drowning in an ocean of emotional bliss
Dripping wet

***

Your Kiss

Placing your lips on mine
Forcefully I pull you into my mouth
Reaching to touch your tongue
Tasting the very essence of you

Our bodies embracing
Heat rising
Hands grasping
Souls extending

Your flavor excites me
Each touch of our tongues I want more of you
Exciting a desire to consume
Inhaling every ounce of your scent

Suddenly grasping the back of your head
I cover your mouth fully
Inhale deeply
Stealing back the breath you took away from me

***

Reflection

Revealed in every special moment
The stark naked truth
Standing alone before your eyes
Overwhelming your body

Filling your mind
Such powerful feelings
Exploding in euphoric release
Life's passion
Too often buried
Deep within you

***

Tears

Your sweetness is sour in my eyes
Each drop descending desperately down my cheek
Searching anxiously for a bitter joyfulness
Seeking hope in despairing lips
Pain controls my excited senses
You devastate me with your affectionate smile
Enjoying your dereliction of my loving heart
All is lost
Burning is my soul on fire

***

Saudade

In the void that silence has created colors, hues
and aromas fill my space
Remembrances of a first smile blinding me with
brilliant light

An initial moment of encounter, when your eyes pierced my veil
Sticking deep into my soul
Such warmth in our embrace that two long lost souls rejoining would feel
How gentle and sweet the song of your voice bending my ear
The welcome invasion of your scent into my nostrils
When exuberance grew between us as your pounding heart raced faster
With sweaty palms in earnest our hands joined tighter
Perfect in our symmetry and synergy
Walking in unison on our new adventure together
Sudden intention pressed with deliberate lips to seal our connection
Slowly rocking intertwined, our magnetic embrace fixed at the hearts
Moist joyfulness lubricating words of expressed need and desire
Surrounded in trust with unguarded affection
When imagination explores the expanse of our greatest fears in delight
Excitement leading our passion unbridled towards ecstasy
Confectioning dreams incomparable from a woven tapestry of dreams unfathomable
Insouciant thoughts exchanging forcefully at lightning's breath

While our burning minds consumed each others delights deep into the night eternally
Now alone I reflect
On that magnificent energy creating power perverse
Wanting nothing but our connection
Knowing it is always mine eternal
But lost from my grasp here and now
Delivering limbo to my anxious tongue
Overwhelmed to a desperate taste of waiting
Accepting my soul love may sometimes walk alone in beauty

***

My love that you're running from

As the rain came on tonight
My heart fell silent
Listening for a word from you in the darkness

It's deafening at times
The silence
My chest feels cold from the sadness in my heart

There are no new messages
Each time I check the Phone
Like I have a nervous tick somehow I keep looking for you

Bob Marley begins to sing in my head

I don't want to wait in vain for your love
Somehow I still see us listening to this song on a road trip together

Being hopelessly in love with you
Falling from such heights
I have to believe you are still my parachute

Why else would I have jumped?
My faith and belief in you
Are the only things keeping me from hitting the ground

What is it like for you?
To fight the love that you feel inside
Blocking all the positive vibrations that we share

How do you handle the silence?
There is no amount of noise
Keeping my mind distracted from wandering back to you

Every action correlates back to you
Each chance to find allegory
No activity is safe from your presence

There is no joy without you
I have become dependent
Now all I can do is wait in vain for you to receive my gifts once again

The day before
Still feels like I received the greatest gift
I hope I get to unwrap you again

Why is it my love
That you are running from
When you know that it is what you want

Why is it my love
That you are running from
When you know you need it now

Why is it my love
You resist so willingly
While it nourishes your soul so completely

It's my love
That is your relief
Running through your veins with total passion

Can you really stay away?
Feeling so amorous
For the love that you're running from

Tears in my eyes burn
Bob sings softly
While I wait for my gift to return

***

Passion

You invade my soul.

No. You know you gave it to me willingly.
Maybe you will realize how I just learned every inch
of its expanse and
Implanted myself permanently.

You suffocate me.

No. You want to take my breath away.
Sooner or later, I try to steal it back.

You tie me in knots.

No. You may have knots in your back.
You know I unravel your feelings.
Start to imagine how I set your emotions free.

You keep me off-balance.

No. You may not be used to being so light and free.
Sure, I can tell you that I remove the weight on
your shoulders.

You confine me.

No. If you limit yourself from being then
I make you feel the choices that exist.

You haunt me.

Yes. Imagine how it feels to love with such haunt.

***

Thundershowers

There was a downpour earlier tonight
The rain came loud, the thunder tight
Each sharp crack began a magnificent boom
I imagined us in the bedroom

Your supple breasts heaving up
My hands reaching to gentle cup
Grasping deliberately at each tweak
Watching you rise to your highest peak

Then fall again and feel your desire
Taking all of me inside your fire
Enjoying your hard and swollen friend
In your soaking wetness until the end

Then a clap of thunder, a smack on your ass
Out jumps a scream and something crass
Your moan bellows with your shape and form
Your body becoming a thunderstorm

Up and down and side to side
You wind your hips with a ticket to ride
Coming to climax as you steadily sway

Each convulsion you shake away

Again I smack your ass with force
This time your moan is dark and hoarse
You come again without control
Feeling all of me filling you whole

As you succumb to the pleasure deep
I release into you while you weep
Tears of joy falling on to me
As we share each other in total ecstasy

***

Submission

Disguised in your eyes are stars of wonderment
Behind them lies your soul
Under thoughtful watch of bright enlightenment
Inspiration makes you whole

Captured now by forthright hand
Determined for your lips
Yielding for illusions grand
Expressed wildly through swaying hips

Succumbing to the taste supreme
Bound silent with muscles weak
Accommodating all actions to extreme
Exultation present from every shriek

Conceding whole in sheer delight
Unconcerned of such position
Acceptance fully for new plight
Jubilant in submission

***

Your lips

Passion releases from your press
So gentle is your touch
In each second connected you express
All relief from day's stress

Locked in heat and fire extreme
Excitement in your clutch
Hesitant your eyes gleam
Filling love supreme

Unlocked are your feelings true
Hidden in dark past
Released from terror expressed new
Glowing bright with sharpened hue

Now I sense your shoulders tremble
Happiness in such fear
From my I eyes do I assemble
Your love so monumental

Communication

I love you
I want you to enjoy an abundant life
I hope to create with you.

Please know
it hurts
when you miss appointments
especially when you set the time

You are forgiven
I just ask
from this point on
you recognize
time is precious

I need your respect for
my time
the same way I
value yours

Going forward
any reason
you may miss a call
just message
you will let me know a time when you are free
even if that means you don't know when

The consideration
important for the other person

receiving

I love you
I do not want simple matters
communication and consideration
to disconnect us
from each other

***

The worth of your mind

Between the walls lives infinite imagination
Not created from within stars
Born instead from superior cataclysms of stars
colliding together
Inspiring the world through each rare unique
thought

Radiating from your smile are the gamma-rays of
its origin
Glowing through your eyes its aura gleams
Malleable to the brutal force of knowledge
Conductive to the heat and electricity of wisdom

Deep inside your layers of complexity
You cradle atoms bonded together that sparkle
Dispersing light in every color
Compressed from millions of years of pressure into
flawless paragons

Hefty in the weight of each carat
Precise with the quality of each cut
Intense for purity of color
Free from any inclusions to its clarity

Resistant to everything but the highest heat and pressure
Hardest to scratch or break
Indomitable in its will to be independent
Disobedient to the weaker mind

Captivating to the appreciating mind
Secured from fleeting interest
Open only to the deepest connection
Penetrating the furthest regions of its mystery

Captured only by an equal or greater power
Yielding to receive an eruption of feelings newly entered
Bursting with limitless energy overflowing sufficiently throughout the space within
Priceless to the mind who falls in love with it

***

7 words

Intensely
Your eyes pierce
into my Heart

Your hands
So eloquently behold
My shoulders

Your thoughts
A poem of
Life's future

Brightly
Smiling you asphyxiate
My naked soul

Unmistakeably
Our hearts grow
As we grow

So rich
Is life
With our future

Seed
Planted firmly
Deep in my heart

Your soul
Radiates love
That I adore

Firmly
In your womb
Passion exists unbridled

Secured
With ravenous greed
For your pleasure

Beautiful
Your soul intoxicates
My total existence

***

True Love

Sweet dreams
wake knowing I look at everyday
with you as a gift
know what I want most
is the privilege to unwrap
the gift you give me of yourself
over and over again
You are my want
mental, physical and spiritual
Your selfishness is my challenge to overcome
in my desire to have your
total possession
total submission

Together I want to explore
the depths of our desires
extents of our imagination
push our limits in all realms
My need for your unbridled passion
lust is only surpassed by my own
unquenchable thirst for your beautiful naked soul
I drink every ounce of your radiance in delight
You excite me
you thrill me
you confound me
you torture me
you vex me
you torment me
you inspire me

such unfathomable heights that I wallow in despair
without your smile
kiss
hug
pleasure
happiness

I am consumed and want to consume
more of you each day until I have devoured you
absorbed all of your essence
as the scent of my existence
No, I will not relinquish my need for you
I will not allow you to let your selfishness destroy
you or us

My demand for your attention
adoration
appreciation
stimulation
sophistication
satiation
sex and soul
exposed
unsure and unwilling
is the oxygen that wakes my senses
ignites the fire within all my blood
accelerates every synapse of my thumping heart
to protect, shield and love you
my most valuable and sacred possession
I wake and sleep with you
my sunrise and sunset

the fire within you
resist submitting to yourself and to me
the burning sense of independence
self-reliance you must demonstrate to yourself
I revel in the fight
the relentless defiance
the uncompromising determination
to be virtuous
knowing that my will looms over you
A foreboding sense of pleasure
ecstasy ever present
to punish you into that submission
you truly need to satisfy your full natural existence
a woman on earth

I want to unleash you from yourself
ride the limitless wave of euphoria
with you throughout eternity
The joy you are inside my being
You invigorate my soul
leave me helpless to my craving
to be lost inside you
relegated to wander ungoverned
within your incalculable folds of luminous passion

I inhale you
leaving nothing to exhale
Love is dull and boring
compared with the energy
you vibrate with me
I bask in that vibration with no ounce of remorse

Bonaparte and Clementine crash in the French Quarter

Bonaparte held his hand steady on the bottom of the steering wheel as he drove the rental SUV along the gulf coast highway. His eyes were fixed on the road ahead with careful determination as he secured his foot on the accelerator surely to keep their speed locked at a comfortable eighty-five miles per hour. Clementine was just beginning to wake from an afternoon nap in the passenger's seat, she had been dozing on and off for the better part of the last several hours and had gone into a deep sleep somewhere between two and three o'clock. It was now four-thirty and she was beginning to feel the growl in her belly as suppertime was approaching. She looked over at Bonaparte who was lost in his thoughts, as usual, probably daydreaming about something work related. He never took time off to just relax completely, even on vacation with her.

"Bumpeeeee, I'm hungry." Clementine whined.

"There's a surprise." Bonaparte replied.

"Can we stop soon? I think I need to pee." Clementine continued.

Bonaparte looked up to see an exit sign and a sign for gas and food one mile ahead. He carefully clicked his blinker on and methodically merged to the right lane after making sure all of his mirrors were clear.

"Yeah sure. There's a gas station and food up ahead. Hopefully, you'll like the food this time." Bonaparte grumbled.

"What's that supposed to mean? Are you calling me a picky eater because there was a hair in my burrito? Well, then I'm a fucking picky eater you fucking asshole!" Clementine blurted. "You know what? Fuckit, I'm not hungry! Keep driving jerkwad!"

"Clue, shut the fuck up." Bonaparte said calmly.

"DON'T TELL ME TO SHUT THE FUCK UP! I'LL SAY WHAT THE HELL I WANT!" Clementine screamed.

Bonaparte gently let his foot off the accelerator and began to merge right to the exit ramp. He let the car slow down on its own and kept the blinker on just to let the clicking sound linger, in hopes it might piss off Clementine some more while he felt her seething glare on his cheek. Straight ahead, Bonaparte could see the gas station sign pointing left about eight-tenths of a mile. He glided the car around the curve and slid into the highway staying in the right lane to pull into the station.

"We need gas. The station looks clean, so you can probably use the restroom if you want." Bonaparte started.

"You just want me to starve don't you. You think I'm a fatass!" Clementine grumbled.

"No Clue, I love your ass just the way it is. I think your ass is perfect." Bonaparte replied.

Bonaparte eased the SUV next to the gas pump, stopped the car and opened the door to jump out.

"Bumppppeeeee?" Clementine chirped.

"Yes Clue?" Bonaparte sighed.

"Can you get me a club soda? My tummy is messing with me."

"Sure Clue. I'll get you a club soda. Anything else?" Bonaparte continued.

"No. That's it. Thank you, Bumpee." Clementine sang.

Bonaparte closed the door and walked into the station's convenience store. There were two other customers roaming the aisles and a television overhead with the local news showing. Bonaparte made his way to the refrigerators in the back and looked through the glass for a club soda. Seeing only ginger ale was available, Bonaparte opened the glass window and pulled out the 20oz Seagrams. Then he grabbed a large Lipton Brisk for himself. He closed the glass door quietly and looked up at the television to see if the weather was available. Seeing nothing but a talking head and the word shooting, he looked ahead towards the clerk's counter and started walking in that direction.

It was hotter than Bonaparte had expected as he walked back out into the open air. More humidity than anything else and Bonaparte was not a fan of the humidity. He hated the stickiness and how it messed with his allergies, plus it always made him feel more sluggish. Bonaparte walked across the pavement to the gas pump where the SUV was parked. Clementine was no where in sight and her handbag was gone. As he pulled the hand pump from its rest, flipped the lid to the gas tank and stuck the nozzle in, the passing thought that Clementine may have run off and left him lingered as he squeezed the handle of the pump to let the gas flow. He shook his head, looked out at the road and smiled.

Clementine's annoying laughter broke the quiet solitude Bonaparte was enjoying. She wasn't in sight anyway, but he recognized her annoying cackle and knew she was doing something to piss him off. Bonaparte glanced over at the meter to see how much money was left to pump and figured Clementine would probably be back by the time he finished. He suddenly realized he hadn't put the bag of sodas in the truck and had kept them in his left hand the whole time.

As Bonaparte glanced around the perimeter of the station looking for Clementine, she suddenly popped around the side the store holding the arm of a large, muscular skin-head.

"Oh, you're such a gentleman Randy, I love that about you." Clementine cooed.

"Well now, a pretty little lady deserves a fine gentleman at her service." Randy smiled.

"Ooh, you know just what to say, you big hunk of stud-muffin." Clementine sang in her lilting voice.

Bonaparte met Clementine's eyes as the two chatting strangers walked toward him. Clementine smiled with evil contempt as she bowed her head. She turned to her companion and grabbed his forearm with both her hands.

"Randy, I'd love to have your number, so we can stay in touch. A girl never knows when she might need a handsome stud to help out with a broken pipe or something." Clementine chimed.

"Here's my card, little darlin. You can call me anytime." Randy replied. Clementine took the card, batted her eyelashes at Randy and smiled as she slowly backed away.

"Thank you, Randy."

Bonaparte watched Clementine walk with her head down back toward his direction and didn't flinch. He felt the gas pump click and the last guzzle drain from the spout and turned to replace the hose to is holster. Screwing the gas cap on and closing the door, he firmly grabbed the door of the truck and jumped into the driver seat and started the engine. Clementine opened the passenger door slowly as Bonaparte was buckling his seatbelt.

"I need to eat Bumpy." Clementine began.

"They didn't have club soda." Bonaparte replied.

"Ugh. Why did we have to take this trip?" Clementine retorted.

"I got you ginger ale instead."

"Fine. Where are we going to eat?"

"Somewhere up the road."

"Fuck you Bumpy."

The ends of Bonaparte's mouth curled upward as he pulled the SUV out of the gas station and began looking for a spot to eat that would satisfy Clementine. He knew the regular local diners would not be satisfactory to her taste, they would have to find a larger chain like an Outback Steakhouse or Crackle Barrel to suit her palette.

The sun was setting on the Gulf leaving a reddish-orange trail of light on the water that invited birds and other sea creatures to follow it over the horizon. Bonaparte was driving in silence while Clementine slept in the passenger seat. Their meal had been uneventful for once, Clementine couldn't find anything to complain about and they ate in relative peace. As they entered the city limits of New Orleans, Bonaparte thought it a good idea to wake Clementine so she could see the city lights with the bright red sky behind it.

"Clue, we're here." Bonaparte spoke softly.

"Mmmmmmm. Bumppeee, why are we still driving?" Clementine stirred from her sleep.

"Look at the sky Clue, I don't think you want to miss this."

Clementine slowly opened her eyes and blinked a couple of times as she looked around.

"Bumpee? Where the fuck are we?" Clementine clamored.

"New Orleans, Clue. We're here." Bonaparte replied.

"We're not here, Bumpee, we're still driving. Here is when you are in your hotel. We are not in our hotel, yet." Clementine snapped back

"Ok. Well the sky is bright red and the city lights are on and I thought you might want to see this for yourself." Bonaparte calmly answered.

Clementine rolled her eyes and starred out the window. The view was spectacular she had to admit, but she wasn't about to give Bonaparte the satisfaction of knowing that.

"You could've let me sleep until we got to the hotel." Clementine snarked.

"I probably should have, you're right." Bonaparte considered.

Clementine swung her left arm and hit Bonaparte square in the ribs. Bonaparte winced slightly but didn't react. Clementine swung again and then tried to smack Bonaparte in the face, but Bonaparte reached in time to grab her wrist as she was mid-slap.

"Easy Clue, I'm driving" Bonaparte calmly stated.

"Fuck you Bumpee, I hate you! Your such an asshole!" Clementine shrieked.

Clementine began to writhe her arm in Bonaparte's firm grip. The more she wriggled the firmer Bonaparte squeezed her arm. His concentration on the road was being challenged by this assault from Clementine and although he had her firmly in his grasp, she was continuing to wriggle and attempting to assault him. Bonaparte looked at Clementine and tried to steady the vehicle as she kept trying to slap him.

"Clue! Stop. I don't want to say it again." Bonaparte said in a stern voice.

"Let me go! Let me go! I wanna get the fuck outta here! Stop the car!" Clementine yelled hysterically.

Clementine lunged forward onto Bonaparte and knocked his hand off the wheel. Bonaparte tried to ease onto the brakes and slow the car, but he had no control of the steering wheel and the car began to spin. Suddenly the SUV was heading toward the median and Bonaparte could not stop the impact. The car slammed into the median with incredible force and Bonaparte and Clementine were greeted with airbags in their face.

"Owwwwwwwwwww. Bumpeeeeeeee. Owwwwwwwwwww." Clementine cried.

Bonaparte shook his head, looked around and then reached over to Clementine and put his hand on her head.

"You ok, Clue?"

"No. My head hurts Bumpee. I think I got a concussion." Clementine replied.

"I'll call for an ambulance. You're gonna be ok, Clue."

Bonaparte reached for his phone and dialed 911. Within a half-hour the police and ambulance arrived and took statements and checked Clementine out thoroughly. A tow-truck came to take the SUV to a repair shop. Bonaparte and Clementine rode in the tow-truck to the shop.

"First time in New Orleans?" The driver began.

"Yes. It's our anniversary." Clementine sniffled.

"Unfortunate start." the driver replied.

The repair shop was dimly lit on the outside and Bonaparte did not see anyone at the desk inside. The driver pulled the truck into the front lot and backed the SUV into a space by the garage. He got out and lowered the car down onto the ground, unhooking it from the truck.

"You can go inside with your bags. There'll be a car here in about twenty minutes to take you to your hotel. You should be able to pick up your car tomorrow afternoon. It don't look to be that much damage."

"Thanks. Let's go, Clue." Bonaparte replied as he pulled their luggage from the SUV.

Clementine walked behind Bonaparte with her head down into the office and sat on the leather chair by the coffee table. She looked around the room and sighed.

"I think I need to go to the bathroom and check myself out." She began.

"Ok Clue. I think it's over there to the left. You ok?" Bonaparte said, looking around.

"I think so."

Clementine found the bathroom after a few wrong turns. She put her bag down on the counter and started sniffling. She grabbed some paper napkins from the dispenser and began to run the water over them to wipe her face. Her sobs grew stronger as she looked at the mascara running down her face and buried her eyes into the napkins. She did not hear Bonaparte come in as she was washing her face and hands.

Bonaparte walked up to Clementine and grabbed her firmly around the neck with his right hand so she could not breathe. She looked up to see him in the mirror as he grabbed her waist with his left hand and started unbuttoning her jeans. Quickly, he maneuvered her pants down and ripped her panties off with a wild yank. Clementine gasped, but she did not fight. She followed the force of his arm down onto the counter and pushed her hips back in anticipation for what she was about to receive. Suddenly, Bonaparte pushed himself deep. She moaned.

"Ohhh. Bumpeee. Yes!"

Bonaparte thrusted harder as he heard Clementine gasp and try to inhale. Slowly, he pulled his hand off her throat and grabbed her shoulder for better leverage. His left hand went up the inside of her shirt as he pushed his fingers across her chest and squeezed firmly on her left breast.

"Yes, Bumpee. Don't Stop. Please don't stop."

Bonaparte's hands roamed freely over Clementine as he stroked faster. He raised his right hand and came down firmly on Clementine right cheek. She howled in delight and moaned again.

"Again. Please Master, again."

Bonaparte smacked her cheek even harder this time. They were both in a frenzy and panting heavy, short breaths. Suddenly, Bonaparte pulled Clementine by the neck up to his mouth and growled in her ear as he released. Clementine moaned and shuttered as she began to convulse uncontrollably and fell onto the countertop. Bonaparte paused for a moment to catch his breath and then slowly pulled out of Clementine. He zipped up and began to walk out of the bathroom.

"Car's waiting outside, Clue." Bonaparte muttered as the door closed behind him.

Clementine rested her head into Bonaparte's chest as the cab drove slowly through the French Quarter. Bonaparte was looking at the lights and the old buildings, mesmerized by everything he saw outside the window. Gently, Clementine reached for Bonaparte's hand and placed hers firmly inside and squeezed.

"Happy Anniversary, Bumpee." Clementine smiled.

"Happy Anniversary, Clue."

www.ingramcontent.com/pod-product-compliance
Lightning Source LLC
Chambersburg PA
CBHW031406040426
42444CB00005B/440